The 'Lion of Rajasthan'

Bhairon Singh Shekhawat

Life & Times of Bhairon Singh Shekhawat

The 'Lion of Rajasthan' : Bhairon Singh Shekhawat (Life & Times of Bhairon Singh Shekhawat)

The 'Lion of Rajasthan'
Bhairon Singh Shekhawat

Life & Times of Bhairon Singh Shekhawat

Compiled & Edited by :
rahul singhal
a concerted effort : **xact**

PENTAGON PAPERBACKS

The 'Lion of Rajasthan' : Bhairon Singh Shekhawat (Life & Times of Bhairon Singh Shekhawat)

Great Personalities : Life Sketch Series-5

The 'Lion of Rajasthan'

Bhairon Singh Shekhawat

Life & Times of Bhairon Singh Shekhawat

Compiled & Edited by :

rahul singhal

a concerted effort by :

xact ad 'n' art studio

Team Leader :

Rahul Singhal & Rohit

Team Members :

Assisted : Daljit Kaur Gaba, Soma Kolay, Ratnakshi, Rinki

Caricatures by : K. V. Gautam

Cover Illustration by : Deepak Kumar

First Published : 2002

ISBN 81 86830 61 8

Published by :

PENTAGON PAPERBACKS

101, AVG Bhawan,
M-3, Cannaught Place
New Delhi - 110 001
INDIA

Concept & Design by :

XACT AD 'N' ART STUDIO

Delhi

Printed at :

Elegant Printers

New Delhi

PENTAGON PAPERBACKS

From Editor

"The 'Lion of Rajasthan' : Life and Times of Bhairon Singh Shekhawat" is a brief life sketch of Sri Bhairon Singh Shekhawat, a man of determination who despite of many odds kept on shining at the top of political galaxy of Rajasthan and is always counted among top leaders of BJP.

This book unfolds the dynamism of Sri Shekhawat's life. The book furnishes an insight into the personality of Shekhawat who is a flag bearer of harmony in politics. For him ideological differences never proved to be a stumbling block in personal relation. It is this quality of Shekhawat, which played its role in shaping the NDA. Above all, the book narrates Shekhawat as a man and catches his finest moments of emotions.

Caricatures have been added in this book to bring forth the various aspects in Shekhawat's life in a more strikingly, lively and interesting manner.

CONTENTS

Bhairon Singh Shekhawat

Introduction

Bhairon Singh Shekhawat has become a household name in Rajasthan. He is popularly known as 'Bhairon Baba' and 'Baba' among his followers. He is counted among top of political galaxies of Rajasthan. Wherever he goes, masses starts chanting in his respect "Bhairon Singh Shekhawat Zindabad" and "***Rajasthan ka ek hi singh- Bhairon Singh, Bhairon Singh***".

He was born to Shri Devi Singh and Smt. Banna Kanwar in Khachriyavas village at Sikar district in 1923. He completed his higher secondary education from Khachriyavas only. Bhairon Singh Shekhawat was married to Smt. Suraj Kanwar and has one daughter. The couple does not have a son. Following his elder brother's footsteps he joined the police service and soon became popular by nabbing notorious robbers.

Shekhawat's interest is in social service. His chief source of livelihood is agriculture. He has been to Europe and US.

Shekhawat's political journey begins from 1952 when the very first election of Independent India was being held to democratically elect people's governments right from the level of centre to that of the states.

By this time Shekhawat had no political linkages. Except his elder brother, Bishan Singh, who was a member of RSS, no other member of his family had any political background. Even Shekhawat recognises this fact and claims; "***The family background I belong to could not have even led me to Sarpanch, leave the question of Indian Vice-President***"

Jansangh offered his brother to contest election from Ramgargha seat. Being in government service, he denied accepting the offer of Jansangha and asked his brother Bhairon Singh Shekhawat to contest the election. Shekhawat contested and won the election. Since 1952 he contested for 11 times, except once, he got elected every time. Since the inception of Jansangha, he held the post of MLA for a long period of time. Emergency brought him into national politics. At that time he was in Rajya Sabha elected from Madhya Pradesh. He spent most of his time in jail instead of Rajya Sabha. In this regard Shekhawat says "***If there were no democracy, I could not have done it and farming would have been the only option left for me.***" And the auspicious time came in 1977 when he for the first time assumed the post of Chief Minister. Since 1977 till the coming of Ashok Gehlot as the Chief Minister of Rajasthan, his political career witnessed many ups and downs.

His fortune of becoming the Chief-Minister of Rajasthan became unfortunate with the return of Congress in 1980,because he was also one of the many victims of Indira Gandhi, who dismissed the state governments. His political personality is so scattering that where his party had to wait for one decade for coming to power, Shekhawat got elected again and again and remained leader of the opposition in assembly. He has been so lucky, that once again he became Chief Minister in 1990 but unfortunately with the demolition of Babri Masjid in 1992, his chief ministership was also demolished by the centre. Within one year in 1993, he again returned to the power as the Chief Minister of Rajasthan and served the state till 1998.

The fact that he is the only Chief Minister of BJP who has successfully completed his tenure, clearly shows his political competency.

Despite of belonging to an extreme, right wing political party, Shekhawat has many good friends belonging to different political galaxies.

From Police to Power

Following his elder brother's footsteps, he joined the police service and soon became popular by nabbing notorious robbers.

Shekhawat's political journey begins from 1952 when the very first election of the Independent India was being held to democratically elect people's governments, right from the level of centre to that of states.

By this time Shekhawat had no political linkages. Except his elder brother, Bishan Singh, who was a member of RSS, no other member of his family had any political background. Even Shekhawat recognises this fact and claims, "***The family background I belong to could not have even led me to Sarpanch, leave aside the question of Indian Vice-President.***"

Jansangh offered his brother to contest election from Ramgargha seat. Being in government service, he denied accepting the offer of Jansangha and asked his brother Bhairon Singh Shekhawat to contest the election. Shekhawat contested and won the election.

From Jansangh to BJP

His brother was a RSS activist, but being in government service, he denied accepting the offer of Jansangha for Ramgardh seat in 1952. But it was Shekhawat who agreed to accept it and threw himself into the fray. Since 1952 he has contested the elections 11 times, and except once, he got elected everytime. Since the inception of Jansangha, he held the post of MLA for a long period of time. Emergency brought him into national politics. At that time he was in Rajya Sabha from Madhya Pradesh. He spent most of his time in jail instead of Rajya Sabha because that time, and Shekhawat says in this regard that "If there were no democracy, I could not have done it and farming would have been only option left for me." And the auspicious time came in 1977 when he for the first time assumed the post of Chief Minister. Since 1977 till the coming of Ashok Gehlot as CM of Rajasthan, his political career witnessed many ups and downs.

His fortune of becoming Chief-Minister of Rajasthan became unfortunate with the return of Congress in 1980,because he was among one of the many victims of Indira Gandhi, who dismissed state governments. Despite of a wave in favour of Indira Gandhi in 1980 elections, in which many stalwarts of opposition could not even save their deposits, Shekhawat won the election from Chabda and became the leader of opposition in Rajasthan state assembly. His political personality is so scattering that where his party had to wait for one decade for coming to the power, Shekhawat got elected again and again and remained leader of opposition in assembly. He has been so lucky, that once again he became CM in 1990 but unfortunately with the demolition of Babri Masjid in 1992 his chief ministership was also demolished by center. Within one year in 1993 he again returned to the power as CM of Rajasthan and served the state till 1998.

The fact that he is the only CM of BJP who successfully completed his tenure clearly shows his political competency.

Despite of belonging to an extreme right wing political party Shekhawat has many good friends belonging to different political galaxies.

"The only religion that will guide my activities will be Raj Dharma."

Nineteen Ninety-Three. Backed by the Marxists and other assorted pseudo-secularists, **the Rao Government introduced two draconian Bills -- the Constitution 80th Amendment Bill and the Representation of People (Amendment) Bill with the dual purpose of banning religion from public life as well as denying political space to the BJP.** The underpinning of these proposed legislations, as in the past, was minority appeasement and crass vote bank politics. The BJP stalled the Bills in Parliament and the debate was deferred, although the Bills were not withdrawn.

The BJP's opposition was articulated by Shri Advani:

"***We strongly object to religion being translated as dharma... for the average Indian, irrespective of whether he is a Hindu, or a Muslim or a Christian, his respective religion is for him an inspiration for righteous conduct. By ousting religion from politics, we will only be weakening the moral base of public life... politics should be cleansed of adharma, not dharma. It should be rid of corruption and criminalisation, not of probity and integrity...***"

Through these Bills, the pseudo-secularists sought to achieve four principal objectives :

- Subvert the basic scheme of elections and allow pre-emptive disqualification;
- Provide constitutional legitimacy to banning organisations;
- Make the state irreligious rather than one which respects all religions equally;
- Allow the summary deregistration of political parties.

Once again Shri Advani took the lead in mobilising public opinion against these draconian, anti-democratic, anti-people measures. He planned a four-pronged yatra, to be led by senior leaders of the party. Thus was born the Janadesh Yatra with the purpose of seeking the people's mandate against the two Bills.

The four yatras began on September 11, 1993, the birth anniversary of Swami Vivekananda, from four corners of the country. Shri Advani himself led the yatra from Mysore; Shri Bhairon Singh Shekhawat from Jammu; Shri Murli Manohar Joshi from Porbandar; and, Shri Kalyan Singh from Calcutta. Travelling through 14 States and two Union Territories, the yatris congregated at Bhopal on September 25 in a massive rally. The Janadesh Yatra was a runaway success.

It was, by all accounts, an unprecedented programme of mass contact; a programme that took the debate on the 'Religion Bills' from the antiseptic drawing rooms of Delhi to the dusty villages of Bharat. Once again, while the BJP's detractors schemed and plotted in the national Capital, the BJP went to the nation's people!

Shri Advani had a tremendous response in Naxalite Telegana. Huge crowds greeted Shri Joshi in Ahmedabad. The tumultuous response to Shri Kalyan Singh in Calcutta prompted The Indian Express to headline its report: 'Red City Turns Saffron", a report which acknowledged, 'the city will perhaps never be the same again." In terrorism-affected Punjab, for the first time in a decade a political party had come out in such a big way: As crowds greeted Shri

Shekhawat, officials thanked him, saying the yatra had helped revive the morale of the administration.

The Bills were never passed. Indeed, its proponents, clearly scared by the public rejection of their dubious move, could not summon the courage to initiate a debate. The adharmic move of the pseudo-secularists was once again defeated by the forces of dharma. The evocative theme of the Janadesh Yatra, "***Loktantra Rakshanaye, Dharmachakra Pravartanaye***". proved a winner.

In the Upper House

During his five decades long political life, before becoming the Vice-President of India, Shekhawat came out of his state Rajasthan just once when he was elected a member of the Parliament for the upper house of the Parliament from Madhya Pradesh. Even in Rajya Sabha he left his marks to be followed by others. A glimpse of his involvement in the Rajya Sabha at the question of upholding dignity of the house is being given here from the records of Rajya Sabha itself.

Rajya Sabha (1974)

Point of Privilege

Casting reflections on the House in a communication allegedly written by the President of a Co-operative House Building Society to Lt. Governor of Delhi.

Facts of the Case and reference to the Committee of Privileges.

On the 10th May, 1974, Shri Bhairon Singh Shekhawat, a member, sought to raise a question of privilege against Shri Jagjit Singh, president, New Friends Co-operative House Building Society, for casting aspersions on the House in a letter dated the 7th May, 1974, alleged to have been written by him to Shri Baleshwar Prasad, the then Lt. Governor of Delhi. While producing a photostat copy of the impugned letter, Shri Shekhawat contended that the language used in the letter, and more particularly the following two sentences written therein amounted to breach of privilege and contempt of the House.

"I have assessed the situation and feel it will not be possible for me and committee to stand the opposition in view of the Court's attitude and its further exploitation in Parliament and papers, unless full support from police and Registrar, Societies is afforded much more than ever."

Since you are busy due to riots in the city, I will give the notice in newspapers only when I get a green signal. It is good that Parliament closes on or before the 13th of May, 1975."

On a motion moved by Shri Shekhawat the matter was referred to the Committee of Privileges by the House.

Findings and Recommendations of the Committee

The Committee of Privileges, after examining **Sarvashri Bhairon Singh Shekhawat** and **Jagjit Singh** and also after persuing the material called for by the Committee from the then Lt. Governor of Delhi and Shri Jagjit Singh, in their Fifteenth Report, presented to the House on the 18th February, 1975, reported inter alia as follows:

(1) ...... the Committee examined the different aspects

of the statement made by Shri Shekhawat in the light of letters received from Shri Jagjit Singh and the Lt. Governor of Delhi wherein both of them had denied having written or received such a letter. The Committee felt that since Shri Shekhawat had neither seen the original letter nor had any knowledge of its present whereabouts and also because of his inability to produce before the Committee the person who had given him the photostat copy of the impugned letter or to give any help to the Committee in the matter, a stage had been reached where it was not possible for the Committee to lay hands on the original letter, even if it existed. The Committee, therefore, had perforce to decide the case on the basis of the materials already before it."

(ii) "After giving its careful consideration to the matter, the Committee did not feel satisfied about the genuineness of the photostat copy of the alleged, letter of 'Shri Jagjit Singh. In view of this, the Committee did not like to examine on merits the question as to whether or not the contents of the alleged letter constituted a breach of privilege or contempt of the House."

(iii) "The Committee, however, felt that any member, who would desire to raise a question of breach of privilege in the House on the basis of any document should be circumspect and should satisfy himself about its genuineness beforehand."

(iv) "In the view taken by the Committee and in the circumstances of the case, the Committee recommends that no further action be taken by the House in the matter and it may be dropped."

Action taken by the House

No further action was taken by the House in the matter

"People had the right to demand and receive details of expenditure on developments works in their villages."

Bold and Outspoken

Shekhawat is known for his soft heartedness. He has a smiling face too. But he could also be bold and outspoken when needed. Sometimes when he deals with members and leaders of his own party he deals strongly. He often did not pause to contemplate the effect of his stands on his political career, and always apposed the fundamentalist attitude of RSS and its attempt to Saffronise the educational curriculum and society.

Shekhawat is a matured and seasoned politician, who always thinks for the betterment and progress of the people and his party. Shekhawat is a politician who knows the art of social engineering. No one better knows the importance of maneuvering in electoral politics. His thought was in conflict with RSS. For RSS, commitment and dedication come before politics. Like Vajpayee, Shekhawat always held a liberal view. At various occasions he argued against views of RSS leaders. Due to being liberal he never felt comfortable with RSS.

A Man of Emotions

Politics is not the only aspect of his life. He is a man of emotions. At various occasions he becomes emotional. He is a very sensitive human being, a quality rarely possessed by today's politicians. He understands and shares the feelings and sufferings of others and also understands the values of regards and disregards.

Before filing his nominations for the post of Vice-President he went to the party headquarter to meet his party colleagues. During his interaction with party colleagues there he became very emotional. There were tears in his eyes wanting to spill over. His voice was shaken too. Tearful eyes and shaken voice were revealing the truth to all of them present there that it was his earning of fifty years of his political life, which is not less than any one else.

Son of the Soil

"Rajasthan ka ek hi Singh-Bhairon Singh,BhaironSingh"

Bhairon Singh Shekhawat has become a household name in Rajasthan. He is popularly known as 'Bhairon Baba' and 'Baba' among his followers. He is counted among top of political galaxies of Rajasthan. Wherever he goes masses starts chanting in his respect "***Bhairon Singh Shekhawat Zindabad***" and "***Rajasthan ka ek hi Singh-Bhairon Singh, Bhairon Singh***".

Besides being party colleague, Bhairon Singh Shekhawat is very dear to Vajpayee. When Vajpayee rang up Shekhawat to convey him the decision to nominate him as NDA candidate for the election of the post of Indian Vice-President. Shekhawat asked Vajpayee amusedly "***Whether you want me to promote or want me to keep out of Rajasthan***". This statement of Shekhawat had loudness.

Shekhawat is a key political figure of Rajasthan. He is like a big Banyan tree before which every body looks like a dwarf in Rajasthan.

Shekhawat is so dedicated to his state that he never contested for Lok Sabha.

Shekhawat was offered the post of Vice-Chairman of the Planning Commission only to be denied by the son of the soil.

Once again Shekhawat was offered for the post of Governor of Tamilnadu. And once again the son of the soil refused to move out of Rajasthan.

Leader of the Masses

To understand the importance of Sri Bhairon Singh Shekhawat in the political arena of Rajasthan, as well as for Bhartiya Janata Party at national level a commentary of Rajiv Shukla is being given here which was written at a time when Shekhawat was confronting rebellion from his own party MLAs in the state and the term of Sri L. K. Advani as national president of BJP was soon to expire. The commentary rightly portrays him as a mass leader.

The Bharatiya Janata Party leadership has done the right thing by deciding to support Rajasthan Chief Minister Bhairon Singh Shekhawat in this, his hour of need.

At the moment, Shekhawat's ministry is precariously poised with 13 legislators having turned rebels, with every possibility of this number swelling in the days to come. Besides having to battle the enemy within, the Shekhawat government is also having to combat the United Front government's efforts to destabilise it. So, at this critical juncture, the BJP leadership ought to back the chief minister and deal firmly with the dissidents.

But once Bhairon Singh Shekhawat manages to recapture the required strength in the assembly and restore order in Rajasthan, he must move towards the national arena. Ideally, once this mess is sorted out, Shekhawat should appoint a party leader of his choice as Chief Minister of Rajasthan and bid farewell to state politics.

The reason for this is simple: Shekhawat, I feel, is the right man to succeed L. K. Advani as BJP president. Advani's term ends this November and, already, there is intense speculation over who will lead the party into the next year.

Two former presidents, Atal Bihari Vajpayee and Murli Manohar Joshi, do not seem to be particularly interested in a second term. Vajpayee is, of course, the party's prime ministerial candidate. So, the list of contenders for the top job, besides Shekhawat, includes Kalyan Singh, Sunder Singh Bhandari, Kushabhau Thakre and Bangaru Laxman.

While Bhandari, Thakre and Laxman are all competent party leaders, none of them enjoys any mass support. Kalyan Singh does have a following in his home state but there is every indication that he would rather be chief minister of UP than BJP president.

So, that leaves Shekhawat. Currently into his third stint as Rajasthan Chief Minister, he is respected by political colleagues and rivals alike. His long stint in Rajasthan has made him indispensable to the BJP's scheme of things in its northern stronghold. But now it is time for him to move on.

In the next few months, Shekhawat should get his house in order, nominate a non-rajput leader, preferably a bania or a jat, as chief minister of Rajasthan, and himself move towards the bigger stage awaiting him. Shekhawat will prove a vital vote-catcher in north India as he enjoys tremendous support among the rajput community.

And the senior BJP leader's political acumen cannot

be doubted. He has earned himself the reputation of being a shrewd political operator, who can be entrusted with the responsibility of leading his partymen and dealing with rival political leaders.

Thus, once the party leadership manages to resolve the Rajasthan crisis, it should take immediate steps to pave the way for Shekhawat's march towards national politics. **The BJP must take full advantage of Shekhawat's abilities and political experience in the crucial months ahead.**

Shekhawat: A Sky Scrapper

Bhairon Singh Shekhawat has been a strong and an old pillar of BJP. He is active in politics since 1952. During these five decade long political career, he made his journey from a Member of Legislative Assembly to Chief Minister (three times) to Vice-President of the Indian Republic. During these fifty years he witnessed many ups and downs in his political career as well as in the political scenario of the state and the nation. During seventies but before emergency, the BJP (then Janasangh) had its hold only in the North India. Even in the North India it was considered a party of Brahmins and Baniyas. At that time Jansangh had just two star leaders Vajpayee in UP and Shekhawat in Rajasthan.

Shekhawat is known for his determination. During the climax of his political career he was confident that he could break Congress anytime in Rajasthan. His determination for development has worked wonders for Rajasthan.

In 1993 assembly election Shekhawat was so popular and influential that when election results were coming most of the newly elected independent Member of the Legislative Assembly and a good number of MLAs from Congress shifted their loyalties to Shekhawat which enabled him to form a government in Rajasthan easily and as a result of which he completed his term successfully.

His influence and hold in national politics can be understood from the fact that when Vajpayee government was formed in 1996 for thirteen days, it was Shekhawat who managed support of MPs from other parties for the Vajpayee government. Once again it was 'Pyar' (PR) of Shekhawat with leaders of other political parties which shaped out NDA.

Despite being held responsible for the defeat of BJP in 1998 Rajasthan State Assembly elections, Bhairon

Singh Shekhawat is such a big name for BJP that he could not be ignored by NDA. That is the reason, he was remembered with due respect. He was invited by NDA for the post of the Vice-President of Indian republic.

Even today his political cult is not less than any one else in BJP.

Like Vajpayee he is also considered liberal in nature, soft-spoken and ever smiling.

Without thinking of any consequences or impact on his political career, he always opposed fundamentalist attitude of RSS and its attempt to saffronise the educational curriculum and society.

The offer to contest the election for the Vice President of India surprisingly comes with the completion of 50 years of public life of Shekhawat. He is a man so devoted to the cause of his own masses, that most of the time he spent in his home State and because of that, Lutyen's Delhi fails to fascinate him. He was born in Khachriyavas village at Sikar district in 1923.He got his education from the same place, but later on he served as police and got fame by nabbing many criminals.

He is so trustworthy that when Chandrashekhar was Prime Minister of India, he asked for the advice of

Shekhawat on Ayodhya issue. Even Laloo Prasad Yadav (Ex. Chief Minister of Bihar, now Rajya Sabha member), sent his two daughters for the admission in Mayo Girls School to Shekhawat. Laloo says about Shekhawat "***He is friend of friends.***" His private life is outside of circumference of politics, that is why it is speculated that he may get more votes as compared to the present arithmetic of the parliament.

Battle back to Health and Power

"It takes your enemy and your friend, working together, to hurt you to the heart," goes a famous line, *"the one to slander you and the other to get the news to you."* Rajasthan Chief Minister Bhairon Singh Shekhawat was battling for life in a US hospital when he heard the news of his adversaries' plans to dislodge him from the Chief Minister's chair. Doctors had suggested immediate surgery to remove a severe blockage in five arteries leading to his heart, providing his adversaries with an opportunity they have dreamt of for over a decade.

It was the second major heart surgery for the 75-year-old Chief Minister, but he battled back to health as gamely as he took on the rebels, single-handedly squashing them with no help from the central leadership of the Bharatiya Janata Party.

It was a golden opportunity for his enemies - and like all popular leaders, he has hordes of them - with the Chief Minister confined to a bed across two oceans for at least one and a half months of enforced absence. Anything was possible.

And indeed, the impossible happened: when Shekhawat left for the US for his surgery, he had 113 votes in the House. He returned home after the so-called rebellion with 115 votes.

The main player in the coup drama was a Janata Dal legislator from Sardarshar, Bhanwar Lal Sharma. Sharma should have known better, he has had ample opportunity to experience Shekhawat's amazing dexterity in realpolitik when he worked as a minister in his last government. But hope, they say, springs eternaly, especially for a legislator who wove himself back into the Janata Dal after his desertion a few years ago. Mr Sharma's political career is chequered: he was elected to the Rajasthan Vidhan Sabha for the first time in 1990 on a Dal ticket when the opposition had fought election jointly. He was inducted in the Cabinet from the Janata Dal quota. But when the BJP withdrew from the partnership with the Dal in the Centre and the Janata Dal consequently walked out of the

Shekhawat government, Sharma chose to remain with Shekhawat, forming a splinter Janata Dal (Digvijai). With the help of this JD(D) Shekhawat retained his chief ministership and Sharma retained his ministership. And when the Shekhawat government was dismissed in the wake of the Babri Masjid demolition, Sharma and his colleagues joined the BJP.

The Dal-turned-BJP legislator was not so helpful when Shekhawat formed his second government in 1993, with the help of independents. Shekhawat was six votes short of an absolute majority in the House of 200 members. His dubious role during that time caused him to be expelled from the BJP.

Ever since then, Sharma had been waiting for his revenge. And the chance came when Shekhawat went abroad for his medical treatment. He tried every trick in the book. According to a FIR filed by a BJP legislator at Keshoraipatan police station, Sharma even offered Rs 20 lakhs to any BJP MLA willing to vote against Shekhawat.

But Sharma was not working in isolation - the Chief Minister has never lacked his share of detractors within his own party, and they were only too willing to be included in any plans that aimed at evicting Shekhawat, and replacing him with another BJP leader. But why should there be dissidence within his own party against a leader who is called by the party high command to quell dissidence in other States? The reasons are predictable: MLAs who want more out of the government in power. The charge against Shekhawat is that, he has given undue importance to the independents who have supported him, even though the party has already 100 members. Aggrieved BJP MLAs feel that Shekhawat is depriving them of their share of the cake, ranging from cabinet berths to less appointments in Boards and Corporations. But those who know Shekhawat well, know that he never bows to pressures, nor is he willing to desert those who helped him in the past. He had promised a respectable deal to the Independents who came to the BJP's rescue when the party's prospects of forming the government were bleak. He now refuses to backtrack on those promises. Nor is he willing to bend his rule barring those with corruption charges from his ministry. Similarly, Shekhawat has stopped MLAs from interfering in postings and transfers, further depriving the MLAs.

Good Governance

Sri Bhairon Singh Shekhawat has always been recognised as a provider of good governance. Even his critics recognise this fact. Some major achievements of Rajasthan government under the leadership of Sri Shekhawat are being given here :

1. Adoption of a new Industrial Policy aimed at rapid industrialization and employment-generation. Increased investment in small-scale sector. Higher investment inflow.

2. Setting up of institutions for imparting technical education. New polytechnics have been opened, including eight exclusively for women.

3. Implementation of special schemes for the welfare of Scheduled Tribes. Increased budgetary allocations and effective targeting of funds. Focus on education and health facilities. Special norms adopted for development projects and the setting up of health care facilities.

4. Introduction of schemes for the welfare and empowerment of women. Special focus on women's education and health. Before the BJP took charge, only nine districts were covered by women's welfare schemes. Today, 31 districts are covered by innovative schemes based on community participation. Steps have been taken to protect the interests of the girl child, infancy through adolescence.

5. Access to primary education in all districts through effective implementation of literacy mission. Special incentives introduced to encourage families to send their children to school and lower the dropout rate;

6. Improvement of villages and urban centres through participatory development schemes. The Government pays part of the expenses; the people contribute the rest.

"Pakistan has failed to respond positively to all deplomatic initiatives of the country to settle related issues."

Mr Bhairon Singh Shekhawat argues "***Pakistan has failed to respond positively to all diplomatic initiatives of the country to settle bilateral issues.***" Mr. Shekhawat strongly put his arguments for a decisive war with Pakistan. He is of the view that war is the only solution to the problem of cross-border terrorism. He firmly believes "***only a decisive war with Pakistan will lead to permanent peace in the region.***"

Some political parties, however, had a different view. They were stressing that all available diplomatic channels should be exhausted first and war should be the last resort. He said in his view all diplomatic efforts had turned out to be an exercise in futility. He said "***the timing of war was a strategic issue to be decided by the Army and the Government.***"

He says India had made all possible efforts to resolve bilateral issues through negotiations as was evident from the Prime Minister, Mr Atal Behari Vajpayee's Lahore bus journey and the Agra summit, but Pakistan had shown no such inclination.

On Terrorism

"There had been no let-up in Pakistan's support to terrorists and suicide attacks on Army personnel and civilians were continuing unabated. The situation had come to such a pass that even the common man favoured a fullscale war to settle the issue once and for all" says Shekhawat.

Expressing concern over the need for the Congress-ruled States to take effective action to curb the activities of anti-national elements in the country, he said in the eventuality of a war, a firm policy to deal with the "enemy within" would have to be put in place and implemented rising above party lines. While the Army and paramilitary forces formed the first and second line of defence, respectively, the support of the people, who backed the two, enabled a country to win wars. There would be no place for saboteurs in the country.

He lamented that the sympathisers of Pakistan, particularly in the Border States like Rajasthan, were having a field day as the state governments were reluctant to use POTO or enforce the ban on SIMI as it went against their policy of appeasement of minorities.

Hundreds of madarsas had sprung up along the border and after the Taliban experience in Afghanistan this should have been taken seriously as the training of "jehad" given in these Islamic institutions would only weaken the country from within. Further, ISI agents were active all over the country and they were mainly indulging in smuggling of drugs and weapons and running fake currency rackets to fund and arm terrorists.

On Infiltration

Shekhawat accuses the Congress and United Front Governments that for their own narrow and selfish reasons they have been deliberately negligent of this problem. The total number of illegal infiltrators from Bangladesh is officially ascertained at over 1.7 crore. The adverse impact of this on our economy and social and political order poses problems of grave magnitude. This cannot be allowed to continue. Shekhawat demands Government to:

1. Take more stringent measures to intercept illegal infiltrators and turn them back. Fencing of the border wherever possible, should be urgently taken

up according to Shekhawat. Border patrolling should also be intensified;

2. Steps should be initiated to detect illegal infiltrators and delete their names from electoral rolls;

3. Maintain a national register of citizens.

Bhairon Singh Shekhawat has been constantly warning the national leaders of the ill consequences of infiltration. A large number of Bangladeshi people have been continuously infiltrating into Indian border since a long period of time. Our country faces various problems caused due to illegal residents.

Shekhawat says "***the population was increasing at a rapid rate, partly due to unchecked infiltration. Besides over 1.7 crore Bangladeshi nationals, lakhs of Pakistanis were staying back in the country after the expiry of the visas.***"

Shekhawat stresses for an urgent need to issue identity cards to citizens to solve the problem of infiltration.

Jai Kisan

AGRICULTURE sustains 71.4 per cent of the Nation's population. It is the mainstay of India's economy and culture. India is blessed with every natural resource needed for sustaining a strong agricultural economy. We have vast cultivable lands, ample sources of water, forests and most importantly, year-long tropical sunlight. We have a large agricultural human resource that has inherited a rich and hoary tradition in farming. It has also acquired the tools of modern science and technology. The combination of these two resources could have transformed Free India into a continental granary. But fifty years of neglect, have severely handicapped the Indian farmer and the entire rural economy. "***Villager is the salt of Indian earth***," said

Mahatma Gandhi. "***Jai Kisan***" said Lal Bahadur Shastri. But in the last five decades, a majority of our ***kisans*** have become poor and harried outcasts in their own country, with no respectful place in the Governments' scheme of things. Today they are on the margins of India's economic, social, cultural and political life.

Sri Bhairon Singh Shekhawat is of the considered view that India will not become a strong, prosperous and confident nation until and unless there is a qualitative improvement in our rural economy and the condition of our kisans. Shekhawat believes that the one-fourth urban India cannot have balanced development without the rapid development of the three-fourths rural India. Hence, rural India is not antagonistic, but complementary and supplementary to urban India.

Against Appeasement

Justice for all, appeasement of none.

Bhairon Singh Shekhawat is a person who prescribes justice for all. He is against appeasement of any individual or community.

Recently the Congress government of Rajasthan decided to build a mosque inside the Mahabhoj temple complex in Asind town of Bhilwara district.

Bhairon Singh Shekhawat said no mosque should be allowed to be built in the Mahabhoj temple complex in Asind town of Bhilwara district.

"***Since there was no mosque inside the temple complex of gurjars there is no question of rebuilding it there,***"

Shekhawat told. Asked whether or not the VHP and Bajrang Dal activists were creating a communal divide in the town over the issue, he said there is nothing like that.

The fact is that about 200 people from outside Rajasthan were staying in Bhilwara district to vitiate the atmosphere, he added.

Secular Shekhawat

"The only religion," Shekhawat declared soon after coming to power, "that will guide my activities will be Raj Dharma." The Chief Minister has indeed strived to live up to his words, and one evidence of this is the enormous confidence that the minorities in the state repose in him. Perhaps he is the only BJP leader in whose house Muslims offer namaz. Shekhawat was the first chief minister of the state to host an Iftaar party, in 1977. The same year Shekhawat not only got the Jama Masjid of Jaipur reopened but spent a considerable sum on its renovation. And among the first things that Shekhawat did when he came to power for the second time was to sanction a Rs 7 crore-beautification plan for the famous Ajmer Dargah.

Shekhawat also ordered free distribution of books to the privately-run madarsas, bending a government scheme that offers free books to the state-run schools. He insisted on making an example by ordering the arrest of his nephew who led an agitation of bus operators. He was equally stern with a delegation of Alwar BJP workers who called on him with a request to release a worker arrested during a communal stir in the town. The plainspoken Chief Minister pointed out to the BJP workers that being from in a ruling party does not give them a licence to create trouble.

Sri Shekhawat is committed to establishing a civilised, humane and just civil order; that which does not discriminate on grounds of caste, religion, class, colour, race or sex. Shekhawat truly and genuinely upholds and practises the concept of secularism consistent with the Indian tradition of 'Sarva panth samadara' (equal respect for all faiths) and on the basis of equality of all. He is committed to the economic, social and educational development of the minorities and takes effective steps in this regard.

For Holy Cause (Cows)

Shekhawat regretfully observes that, despite Article 48 of the Constitution, millions of cows and cow progeny are slaughtered every year, most of them for export, thereby causing irreparable damage to agriculture and villages. Keeping in view Article 48, Shekhawat advocates to :

1. Impose a total ban on the slaughter of cows and cow-progeny, including bulls and bullocks and prohibit all trade, including export (State as well as private) in beef.

2. Create a policy that will result in improved cattle breeding.

3. Exempt the income of Goshalas and Pinjrapoles from tax.

Shekhawat recognizes the fact that from times immemorial, cow-protection has remained one of the basics of the Indian culture and Indian agriculture and it is on the patient back of the cow and its progeny that the entire structure of Indian agriculture rests. Over seven crore animals are employed in farming operations in Indian villages, more than 80 per cent of the rural transport needs are met by the bullock cart. Our livestock also provides an effective protection against environmental degradation, believes Shekhawat.

Roop Kanwar and Shekhawat

Shekhawat did not mince his words when condemning sati after Roop Kanwar was immolated in Deorala. At the time of the sati incident Shekhawat was in New York. The first thing he did on his return was to go to Doral, climb up on a dais and upbraid the villagers for their savagery, calling it "a slur on the Rajput community." Sitting in the audience was a staunch believer in sati, the late Kalyan Singh Kalvi. Shekhawat is a man who believes the devil must be given his due.

Shekhawat has always been in favour of the legislation for the reservation of 33% of the seats in Parliament and State Assemblies for women; plans for providing free education for girls upto college level, including professional courses, so as to better empower women. He is also in favour of setting up a Development Bank for women entrepreneurs in the small scale and tiny sectors.

Hum Do Hamare Do

He is role model for today's people in general and a politician in particular, as far as setting the personal example of family planning is concerned. Shekhawat has just one daughter.

He has been known to publicly praise Sanjay Gandhi for his family planning and afforestation programmes. "The only thing wrong with Sanjay Gandhi's programmers was the style of their implementation," he says.

Not surprisingly, Rajasthan was the first state to introduce a law banning all candidates with more than two children from contesting local elections.

Shekhawat is for making population control a People's Movement. Shekhawat views India's runaway population growth with all the concern it calls for. India's population is set to overtake that of China unless the growth rate is checked and then reversed. The danger of a runaway population growth is there for all to see: A rapidly expanding population means a slower rate of economic growth at which development can be effected. While India was one of the first countries in the world to recognize the need to control the growth of its population in order to ensure a better distribution of the fruits of development, successive Union Governments have failed in the implementation of this important programme. Excesses during the Emergency have given way to complacence and dangerous negligence. Sri Shekhawat is for putting population-related issues, including family planning, firmly back on the national agenda. He believes that the country's runaway population growth can be arrested and rolled back through increased awareness, facilitating access to family planning measures, persuasive Government policies and rapid development-it is an universally acknowledged fact that "***development is the best contraceptive***". Shekhawat knows it very well that Government alone cannot fulfill this gigantic task. The Government's efforts must be supplemented by a vigorous people's movement. In addition, Sri Shekhawat proposes to:

1. Formulate a National Population Policy by acting

on the reports of the National Development Council and the Swaminathan Committee. This Policy will seek to bring the population growth close to stabilization by the year 2010.

2. Provide incentives to those who opt for the "two-child" norm and higher incentives to those who embrace the "single-child" norm.

3. Take all measures for reducing infant mortality rates and improving child health.

4. Promote women's education, employment and empowerment since these can be effective means of population control as they will allow women a decisive role in regard to their reproductive health and family planning.

5. Introduce disincentives which will apply to all sections of society in order to discourage large, unsustainable families.

6. Ensure universal access to family planning information and quality contraceptive facilities by involving Non-Government Organizations and promote awareness among the people, especially women, through counselling, educational programmes and widest use of modern multi-media capabilities.

7. Introduce family planning methods and facilities that will allow women greater freedom of choice without imperiling their health, as well as support research relating to these methods.

8. Encourage women to seek reproductive health services as well as launch a special campaign to educate local communities about negative practice.
9. Offer a special incentive in the form of a fixed deposit that will mature in 21 years for those couples who have only a girl child or those who adopt a girl child under a "***Dattak Putri Yojana***".
10. Make family planning an integral part of our development policies to ensure widest applicability of these incentives and disincentives and provide motivation for a small family norm; and,
11. Ensure that the legal age of marriage is strictly implemented.

Right to Information

TRAVELLING through the arid, undulating land around Beawar in south Rajasthan is like traversing a campaign map marked with historic revolutionary battles. The names of villages and small towns huddled in the folds of the Aravallis recalls scenes of a very different kind of engagement, but which will equally go down in history. Here local villagers have successfully confronted and exposed misrule non-violently; the only weapon they have used is information.

It all started when a small band of social activists joined hands in the late 80s to form the Mazdoor Kisan Shakti Sangathan (MKSS). They soon won confidence by living in the area and identifying themselves with local causes. Like the town of Bhim, where the MKSS set up a fair price shop to bring down prices. Or Lutyana where Shankar Singh, the bard of the campaign, was born. Or Devdoongri, where former IAS officer Aruna Roy lives in a mud hut and from where she and her small team has charted the course of the movement.

The scale of corruption unearthed, even in a small corner of Rajasthan, is mind-boggling. It shows why rural India remains poverty-stricken despite the thousands of crores supposed to be spent on development. The cutting edge of the Right To Information Movement is the **Jan Sunwai** (public hearing) where villagers assemble to testify whether the public works detailed in official bills and vouchers secured by them actually exist. The occasion itself is an impressive demonstration of direct local democracy, with officials invited to be present.

Beawar was the scene of a major engagement in April 1996. A revealing **Jan Sunwai** was followed by a 40-day dharna in which activists were fed and sheltered by the public. Milk and vegetables were distributed daily. Another 40-day dharna was organised in Jaipur. The demand got publicity throughout the country and could no longer be ignored.

At that time Bhairon Singh Shekhawat was the chief minister of Rajasthan. The Rajasthan Government under his leadership responded immediately. The then Chief Minister Bhairon Singh Shekhawat announced that people had the right to demand and receive details of expenditure on development works in their villages. Transparency orders were immediately issued to officials. Right to Information Bills were passed by Rajasthan State legislature. Later on five more state legislatures passed Right to Information Bills.

A Central Bill in New Delhi went through several drafts and is currently before a parliamentary committee. Three months after initial moves taken by Shekhawat in the direction of granting the people Right To Information, in July 1996 politicians, jurists, former bureaucrats, academicians and others joined in, demanding Right To Information legislation at a conference in New Delhi. A committee headed by Justice P.B. Sawant was authorised to draft a model Bill.

In 1996, nobody at Beawar could have hoped that the Right To Information Movement would spread so fast. Its fifth anniversary was celebrated soon after the epoch-making Janawad **Jan Sunwai**. Nearly five hundred participants registered, with groups coming from distant States. Citizens contributed local hospitality, and a local youth group took time off from visiting poor patients in hospitals to welcome visitors at the railway station. A group of fifty singers and drummers from Sawai

Madhupur enthralled the gathering with a chronicle of the Movement. Nothing could have established the unique popular roots of India's Right To Information Movement more firmly. One and all praised the invaluable role played by Bhairon Singh Shekhawat in the direction of granting Right To Information to people.

Managing like Managers

Shekhawat's financial management skills are also considerable, earning him the reluctant praise of the then deputy chairman of the Planning Commission Mr. Pranab Mukherjee.

To the discomfiture of State Congress leaders, Mukherjee and other Congress leaders from the Centre repeatedly praised Shekhawat for his expert running of the State.

When he became the Chief Minister of Rajasthan, the state was known as a Bimaru state. He took the state out of this condition. His government did its best for rural development, poverty eradication and also much have been achieved in the field of education and industry. During his tenure poverty declined down from 26% to 16%, literacy rate went from as low as 28% to 65%. During the decade of 90's, only two state's rate of economic development went up, one was Madhya Pradesh and other was Rajasthan. During 1991-92 to 1997-98, economic growth rate of Rajasthan was 6.2% as against 4.5%. of early decades. He prepared and initiated many projects and schemes of developments. We launched many programmes for poverty eradication which got wide spread recognition in the state. His government started "Food for work" programme, which was a very positive step and proved to be a milestone to do away with unemployment.

Shekhawat is to continue with the reform process, but with a strong Swadeshi thrust to ensure that the national economy grows on the principle that India shall be 'built by Indians'. He is used to reappraise and revitalise reforms through giving primacy to removal of unemployment, and to an accelerated development of infrastructure, particularly energy and power production. He advocates for a GDP growth rate of 7-8% bracket, and control deficits - fiscal and revenue. He is also in favour of enactment of a Fiscal Responsibility Act. Shekhawat is for all such steps that would expedite implementation of policies and programmes in accordance with our national interests; and give to the entire national development efforts a humane face with total eradication of poverty as the ultimate goal. For this '**Berozgari Hatao**' - eradicate unemployment - is his call. Swadeshi is not reinventing the wheel according to Shekhawat. It means facilitating the domestic industry to gain enough muscles to compete with the multinationals in the local and global markets. He wishes domestic companies to flourish and acquire a Trans National status. At the same time the country cannot do without **Foreign Direct Investment** because besides capital stock it brings with it technology, new market practices and most importantly employment. Our target according to Shekhawat should be to achieve at least $ 10 billion per year which will commensurate with our growth objectives. The old leftist approach sought complete state control of industry while the rightist approach wanted to leave everything to the market. He rejects both. Government and industry must work together to achieve key objectives aimed at enhancing the dynamism of the market with effective and effficient regulatory mechanisms; believes Shekhawat. In fact the issue is not about capitalism or socialism, nor is it about market or less state. It is about better society, about improving the way citizens can demand and obtain all sorts of public goods. It is about dignity for all. He firmly resolves that poverty should be relegated to history like slavery, colonialism, small pox and cholera and one must meet the challenge of mobilising resources for that by undertaking the challenge of restructuring priorities and mainstreaming these priorities into new programmes of pro-poor growth and redistribution towards poverty eradication - That is how Shekhawat plans to eradicate absolute poverty within this generation and he strongly feels that it is feasible and affordable infact, it is a moral imperative which one must not miss.

Shekhawat is for carefully analysing the effects of globalisation, calibrate its process by devising a timetable to suit our national conditions and requirements so as not to undermine but strengthen the national economy, the indigenous industrial base and the financial and services sectors.

Shekhawat is in favour to earmark 60% of the Plan Funds for agriculture and effect public investment in agriculture, rural development, irrigation and by diverse incentives, including tax shelters, achieve a quantum leap in agricultural production so that agriculture, horticulture, forestry, food processing, fisheries and so on become the vehicles for growth resulting in an enhancement of the purchasing power of the people. Effective crop insurance schemes should be introduced. Special efforts should be made in Animal Husbandry, Dairying, particularly in respect of Cow and its progeny. This is one of the routes to generating employment, thus eradicating hunger and poverty in rural as well as urban areas. Subsidies of all kinds should be implemented in such a manner as to maximize benefits to all sections of the agricultural population. Development of medium and small scale irrigation projects shall receive priority attention; emphasis for investment should be in accordance with the potential development.

Shekhawat is in favour of a National Water Policy which provides for effective and prompt settlement of disputes and their time-bound implementation. Time-bound steps to link Ganga - Cauvery rivers and Setu Samudram Canal Project should be undertaken according to Shekhawat.

Shekhawat is for increasing the national savings to 30% of the **Gross Domestic Product** by appropriate incentives and through motivation; encourage Foreign Direct Investment in core areas so that it usefully supplements the national efforts and discourage FDI in non-priority areas.

Shekhawat is for comprehensive study of the financial, technological and social security requirements of the self-employed and unincorporated sector; also constitute a Development Bank to promote this largest segment of the national economy which, too, has great employment and self-employment potential. Further, in addition to financial support institutions other institutional systems should be brought for providing services, technology and marketing facilities for artisans, the small-scale, village, khadi, powerloom, handloom, handicrafts and such other industries. This and the Agriculture sectors are an untapped source with unlimited scope for generation of employment according to Shekhawat.

Shekhawat is for a major thrust to infrastructure development, particularly energy and power, by recommending public expenditure in the sector. Towards this one could access long-term funds in the national and international markets, remove administrative bottlenecks, reverse the slowdown in this critical area of national economy thus giving a fresh impetus to growth and private Sector participation will be encouraged, says Shekhawat.

Shekhawat is of the view that a review of all laws and regulations relating to industry should be undertaken so as to free it from bureaucratic control; institute a system of voluntary compliance with laws, including tax laws; ensure speedy redressal of industrial sickness; arrange for meaningful interaction between industry and government; and revive the capital market as a viable and transparent mechanism for raising capital. He is also for expediting comprehensive reform of the **Public Sector Undertakings**, including restructuring, rehabilitation and divestment.

Shekhawat is of the opinion that the Government

should focus on specific products in specific growth areas for exports and announce specific packages for horticulture and floriculture EoUs. He intends to strongly support attempts to build a system of trade and economic cooperation through expanded Global System of Trade Preferences (GSTP) among developing countries. He is in favour of asserting more robustly India's national interests, especially at the review conference of the **World Trade Organisation**. A healthy commodity exchange system should be established to be managed in an autonomous way, according to Shekhawat.

Shekhawat is to take labour, both organized and unorganized, an equal and proud partner in the production of the nation's wealth and in its progress. Laws relating to equal pay for equal work for men and women shall be strictly implemented, asserts Shekhawat.

Recognizing the Right To Work of every citizen, the main thrust of any government should be: '**Berozgaari Hatao**' (Eradicate Unemployment), argues Shekhawat. As against the present trend of jobless growth, the government should measure growth by generation of gainful employment. Our new investment and institutional thrust to agriculture, the self-employed, the unincorporated sector, infrastructure development and housing will act as the vehicles for massive employment creation at all levels, claims Shekhawat.

Any responsible government must embark upon strategic pro-poor policy in terms of which those livin below the poverty line are not to be pitied but treated as net resource replete with their own ideas and experienc well in tune with local conditions. Every effort should b made to provide them work locally and ensure tha schemes for their welfare are competently and honestl administered. They themselves should be treated a participants and facilitators in this noble venture. Th services of NGOs, well versed in this field and, preferabl originating locally, should also be enlisted whereve considered necessary, according to Shekhawat.

Shekhawat is for ensuring food security for al create a hunger-free India, and reform and improve th Public Distribution System (PDS) so as to serve th poorest of the poor in rural and urban areas.

Any government should spare no efforts to ensur that potable drinking water is available to all villages. Ag old and traditional methods of water utilisation, in bot rural and urban areas, should receive urgent attentio opines Shekhawat.

Shekhawat is committed to a total eradication o illiteracy. He is for formulating and implementing plans t gradually increase the governmental and non governmental spending on education upto 6% of th GDP: thus to provide education for all. He is fo mplementing the constitutional provision of making primary education free and compulsory upto 5th standard. Our aim is to move towards equal access to and opportunity of educational standards upto the school leaving stage. We shall strive to improve the quality of education at all levels - from primary schools to our universities, says Shekhawat.

Shelter is a basic human requirement that needs to be met on a priority basis. Shekhawat is, therefore, committed to evolving a National Housing and Habitat Policy in consultation with State Governments, aimed at providing Housing for all. The emphasis should be on the benefit to the poor and the deprived, according to Shekhawat.

"Only a decisive war with Pakistan will lead to permanent peace in the region."

Secret of Success: 'Pyar' (PR)

For a BJP Chief Minister to earn the respect of Congress heavyweights is not a mere fluke of chance or temperament. Shekhawat's skills in public relations is perhaps the secret of his success. Every visitor to the Chief Minister's residence, high and low, is taken to his living room. An acquaintance from a far-flung village once landed up to meet him late at night. Shekhawat not only heard him out, but also sent his own car and driver to drop the villager at the bus-stand. It is gestures like this that has built him a base that neither foe nor friend can hope to topple in his lifetime.

Even Congress MLAs have felt his generosity. One

Congress legislator who approached him for medical assistance for a surgery was overwhelmed when the assistance arrived without prompting at her doorstep. Another Congress leader, a former minister, found a state helicopter at his door in the village to carry him to the state capital when he fell ill. And his attentions are not limited to leaders alone. Shekhawat is often seen in the state-run SMS Hospital, paying calls on lesser mortals and even arranging for their treatment. In such small deeds lie great power. Shekhawat has completed ten years in power, a record broken only by the late Mohan Lal Sukhadia.

Despite of belonging to an extreme right wing political party Shekhawat has many good friends belonging to different political galaxies.

He is so trust worthy that when Chandrashekhar was Prime Minister of India he asked for the advice of Shekhawat on Ayodhya issue.

Even Laloo Prasad Yadav (Ex.CM of Bihar) now Rajya Sabha member, sent his two daughters for the admission in Mayo Girls School to Shekhawat. Laloo says about Shekhawat "He is friend of friends." His private life is one side of circumference of politics that is why it is speculated that he may get more votes as compared to the present arithmetic of the Parliament.

In Red China

In October 2001 Bhairon Singh Shekhawat led a five-member party delegation to China.

A report of The Hindu
India seeks just end to border row with China
29 October 2001

The BJP has said that India-China relations should not become "hostage to past aberrations" and stressed New Delhi's interest in seeking a mutually-acceptable solution to the boundary issue. The senior party leader, Mr. Bhairon Singh Shekhawat, made the point during discussions with China's Communist Party leaders here. "There have been some aberrations in our relationship but we must overcome the problems and find mutually-acceptable solutions," Mr. Shekhawat, who is leading a five-member party delegation to China, told the vice-chairman of the Standing Committee of the National People's Congress, Mr. Jiang Zhenghua. The BJP general secretary, Mr. Sunil Shastri, said Mr. Shekhawat had informed the Chinese leadership of India's desire to find a fair solution to the boundary issue.

Empowering States

The Government of India appointed a Special Task Force on Devolution of Powers to States, under the Chairmanship of Shri Bhairon Singh Shekhawat, to examine and recommend measures for devolution of additional financial powers to the States and additional or alternative means by which States can raise more resources. The recommendations of the report submitted by the task force were examined in consultation with the RBI.

The distinction between plan and non-plan expenditures in our budgetary system has created several problems. It has led to an excessive focus on so called plan expenditures with a corresponding neglect of items such as maintenance, which is classified as non-plan. Various bodies, including the Finance Commission, have advocated the elimination of the plan and non-plan distinction in the budget. It was proposed to constitute a Task Force, including representatives of Planning Commission, Finance Ministry, Comptroller and Auditor-General of India and State Governments to examine these issues in a comprehensive manner and to make recommendations for a functionally viable and more focussed presentation of government expenditure in the budget.

A related problem is the proliferation of Central Sector and Centrally Sponsored Schemes over the years. There is a need to rationalise these, with the objective of reducing overlaps and duplication, modifying procedures and norms and making them more easily accessible to the intended beneficiary. The Task Force will also advise on this issue.

"If there were no democracy, I could not have done it and farming would have been only option left for me."

Vice-President

This is a call from founder of the state's biggest newspaper 'Rajasthan Patrika' and his close friend Karpoor Chand Kushil. "When are you leaving for Delhi?' Shekhawat replied,"tomorrow". Presupposing that Ex-Chief Minister and leader of opposition in the state assembly will stay at the state guest house as before, Kushil asked "where will you stay? At Rajasthan house?". "I could be anywhere. May be with Vajpayee or Advani." Now it was Shekhawat's turn to ask a question,"***Tell me, where does Vice-President of India stay?***"

A few weeks later he shifted to India's Vice-President's official residence at 6, Maulana Azad Road, Delhi.

Shekhawat was leaving for Delhi to file his nomination papers for the post of Vice-President of India as a National Democratic Alliance candidate. It is possible that Shekhawat might not know the residence of Vice-President of India. His becoming the Vice-President of India coincides with his completion of fifty years in public life. Despite of a five decade long political inning if he is not aware of less known symbols of Lutiyen's Delhi its just because he spent most of his time in his own State.

For the National Democratic Alliance, the election of the new Vice-President was a crucial exercise. Strategy managers of the ruling alliance were clear about their plan of action. They choose a person with confirmed BJP credentials. It was veteran Rajasthan leader, Bhairon Singh Shekhawat.

At one stage, the possibility of accommodating the Telugu Desam was mooted, obviously to compensate it for the loss of Speakership, but nothing was heard of it, of late. The members of the two Houses of Parliament chose the Vice-President and the NDA had a safe majority. This was evident during the voting on POTO, at the joint sitting of the two Houses. Given this line-up, the NDA the BJP, in particular saw no need for a consensus. A consensus could involve give and take but the BJP was in no mood for it. Even in the case of the Presidential election, where the NDA had a slight lead in the electoral college, no attempt was made for a meaningful dialogue, and, in the final analysis, the ruling side presented the Opposition with a fair accompli under the facade of consultations. There are no real compulsions in the present case to take the Opposition into confidence.

The NDA made no secret of the unilateral approach it had in mind. On the eve of the presidential election, it spurned suggestions for a package deal on the two high offices. And now, after having outmaneuvered the Opposition in the choice of the President, it will not let others have say in the candidate for the number two posts. With that, the BJP will complete the process of cornering key positions at the Centre. It began with securing the office of the Speaker for Manohar Joshi, member of its closest ally, Shiv Sena. Then came the nomination of A.P.J. Abdul Kalam for the Presidency. His success in the election was a foregone conclusion. True, he is one of the most distinguished technocrats the country has produced, coming into the limelight over four years ago with the nuclear tests, shortly after the assumption of office by the BJP-led coalition, as also with the development of missiles. That may have been one of the considerations that weighed with the BJP in fielding him for the Presidency.

Dr. Kalam, beholden to the BJP for his nomination, it was felt, may not be unhelpful in a difficult situation in the future. In practice, it may not work that way. Dr. Kalam, essentially a non-politician, may not compromise on judgmental independence but that is a different story. Had the BJP seniors not been keen on the choice of "our man," they would not have gone back on their earlier proposal to elevate the Vice-President, Krishan Kant. And the recent reshuffle of the Union Cabinet if at all there was an underlying method, it was the calculation for consolidating the BJP.

The choice of the presiding officer of the Rajya Sabha was extremely important to the BJP. In this House, the NDA was heavily outnumbered and they rightly choose Bhairon Singh Shekhawat for the post of Vice-President of India.

Life and Politics

Excerpt of an interview with Kumar Rakesh after being nominated for the candidature of Vice-President of India by the ruling N.D.A.

You are shifting from state politics to centre. How do you feel?

It is right that by now I have been active in state politics.Now I am taking a responsibility where one should be above partyline.And I"be. I'll try to create and maintain a healthy atmosphere in the house. I will see that the country moves into the right direction and gets benefitted as a whole . The post of Indian vice president is of great responsibilities. I will deliver with full honesty and integrity.

Why you did not move to central politics by now? Why you confined yourself to the state politics?

I have said it so many times that it's the party who decides for me .The party has been doing it . I do not do it myself . I am a disciplined soldier of the party . The decision of this time is also a party decision . It is not my decision. And I humbly carry out their decisions.

Don't you think that it will effect the party in the state ?

I don't think that it will effect the party in the state. Our party is based on caders. Our party is run by collective leadership.

All will work together.They have been working together in the past.

How do you perceive your role in the development of your state ?

When I became the CM of Rajasthan,the state was known as the Bimaru state.I took the state out of this condition.Our government did its best for rural development, poverty eradication and also much have been achieved in the field of education and industry. During my tenure poverty declined down from 26% to 16%, literacy rate went from as low as 28% to 65%. During the decade of 90's, only two state's rate of economic development went up, one was Madhya Pradesh and other was Rajasthan. During 1991-92 to 1997-98, economy growth rate of Rajasthan was 6.2% as against 4.5%. of early decades. I prepared and initiated many projects and schemes of developments. We launched many programmes for poverty eradication which got wide spread recognition in the state. Our government started "Food for work" programme, which was a very positive step and proved to be a milestone to do away with unemployment.

What do you think about Ashok Gehlot's Government?

Gehlot government is no where except news papers. Could you please tell me any other achivement of Gehlot government except contruction of flyovers. In contrast to it, growth rate has gone down from 6.7% to nearly 0% of the state.

But people and observers believe that BJP as a opposition party in the state assembly is not

performing effectively?

This allegation is baseless. We have disclosed the policies of government. We have awakened farmers students, businessmen and common people about their rights and have been doing it continuously State leaders will continue to do it in the future.

But could regional leaders of BJP will retain this fervour and craze after you become Vice-President of India?

Yes, of course, they will be. In our party there are both kind of leaders youth and seniors. There are many experienced leaders in the state. They will continue their fine work.

It is being heard that central minister Vasundhara Raje is to be selected for the state presidentship of BJP?

Yes, I have heard as well. If it is so, it'll be good for the state.

It is being said that it is you who nominated Vasundhara Raje for the post?

Why will I do it? I have not nominated her. It is the

party who has to decide. It's a party decision. Who am I to take this decision or impose it?

Do you believe that BJP will come back in power in the next assembly election?

If you ask me I cann't say at present. What I can say is that Congress will not come back in power. I am 78 years old. I have gone through heart surgery twice and Angioplasty once. Now I am going to take a new responsibility. So, it is state leaders who could say about this.

What will happen to state BJP in your absence?

Leaders emerge from masses. They are not made. Talking about second generation leaders will be dishonesty. Who inspired me to become a leader? I hail from a peasant family. There was no political personality in my family.

What do you think about morality in politics? Has any change taken place?

Politics can not be seperated from society. It's just not possible. Whatever changes take place in society from time to time will have its reflection in politics and will be visible.

Do you have any grievances with life? Is there an[y] unfulfilled dreams?

No grievances, no unfulfilled dreams and n[o] desires. I have lived one chapter of my life in totalit[y]. And I have done my best to lead life without an[y] hassles.

You have accepted party's decision for the post of Vice President. But before this you didn't accept party'[s] offer for Deputy Chairman of Planning Commissio[n] and Governor of Tamilnadu?

That was a different time. This is not the same. It is [a] matter of time.

"Our development work was overshadowed by the onion factor. Pyaj hamare peeche pada tha (The onion was after us). The people have rejected the party, not me."

"I will see that country moves into the right direction and gets benefitted as a whole."

A Brief Chronology of Events in Bhairon Singh Shekhawat's life

A Brief Chronology of events in Bhairon Singh Shekhawat's Life

- *On October 23, 1923, Shekhawat was born to Sri Devi Singh and Smt. Banna Kanwar at Khachariyawas village of Sikar district.*
- *In 1952, he became MLA for the first time from Ramgarh.*
- *In 1957, he became MLA from Siri Madhopur.*
- *In 1962, he became MLA from Kisan Pol.*
- *In 1967, he became MLA from Kisan Pol (Jansangh).*
- *In 1972, he contested but lost (Jansangh).*
- *In 1973, he was elected for Rajya Sabha from Madhya Pradesh (Jansangh).*
- *In 1975, during emergency he was send to jail.*
- *In 1977, he became MLA from Chabda (Janata Party).*
- *In 1977, he was elected as Chief-Minister of Rajasthan for the first time*
- *In 1980, Indira Gandhi dismissed his government*
- *In 1980, he was elected MLA from Chabda (BJP).*
- *In 1980, he was elected leader of opposition of Rajasthan state assembly (BJP).*
- *In 1985, he was elected MLA from Nimbadha (BJP).*
- *In 1985, he was elected leader of opposition of Rajasthan state assembly (BJP).*
- *In 1990, he was elected MLA from Dholpur (BJP).*
- *In 1990, he was elected for Chief Minister of Rajasthan for the second time.*
- *In 1992, his government was dismissed after the demolition of Babri Masjid.*
- *In 1993, he was elected MLA from Bali (BJP).*
- *In 1993 he was elected for Chief Minister of Rajasthan for the third time (BJP).*
- *In 1997, Visited US for heart surgery.*
- *In 1998, Survived rebellion of MLAs against his government.*
- *In 1998, he was elected MLA from Bali (BJP).*
- *In 1998, he was elected leader of opposition of Rajasthan state assembly (BJP).*
- *In October, 2001 he led a five-member party delegation to China.*
- *In August 2002 most probably he becomes Vice-President of the Indian Republic (NDA).*

On October 23, 1923, Shekhawat was born to Sri Devi Singh and Smt. Banna Kanwar at Khachariyawas village of Sikar district.

In 1952, he became MLA for the first time from Ramgarh.

In 1957, he became MLA from Siri Madhopur.

In 1962, he became MLA from Kisan Pol.

In 1967, he became MLA from Kisan Pol (Jansangh).

In 1972, he contested but lost (Jansangh).

In 1973, he was elected for Rajya Sabha from Madhya Pradesh (Jansangh).

In 1975, during emergency he was send to jail.

In 1977, he became MLA from Chabda (Janata Party).

In 1977, he was elected as Chief-Minister of Rajasthan for the first time

In 1980, Indira Gandhi dismissed his government

In 1980, he was elected MLA from Chabda (BJP).

In 1980, he was elected leader of opposition of Rajasthan state assembly (BJP).

In 1985, he was elected MLA from Nimbadha (BJP).

In 1985, he was elected leader of opposition of Rajasthan state assembly (BJP).

In 1990, he was elected MLA from Dholpur (BJP).

In 1990, he was elected for Chief Minister of Rajasthan for the second time.

In 1992, his government was dismissed after the demolition of Babri Masjid.

In 1993, he was elected MLA from Bali (BJP).

In 1993 he was elected for Chief Minister of Rajasthan for the third time (BJP).

In 1997, Visited US for heart surgery.

In 1998, Survived rebellion of MLAs against his government.

In 1998, he was elected MLA from Bali (BJP).

In 1998, he was elected leader of opposition of Rajasthan state assembly (BJP).

In October, 2001 he led a five-member party delegation to China.

In August 2002 most probably he becomes Vice-President of the Indian Republic (NDA).

Cartoonist's Corner

Shekhawat in childhood

He completed his Higher Secondary education from Khachriyavas at Sikar district.

He started his career in police service.

His political journey began in 1952 when he became and MLA.

Later he became a Rajya Sabha member.

During Emergency, he was detained.

After emergency, he became Chief Minister of Rajasthan.

His government was dismissed by Mrs. Gandhi.

He again became Chief Minister but was dismissed after Babri demolition.

One year later, he formed the government and completed the full term.

His Party lost Assembly Polls in 1998 due to Onion Price Rise.

He has friends cutting across political lines.

Bhairon Singh Shekhawat is considered a down-to-earth leader.

Most probably Shekhawat will be Vice-President of India.